The Victorious Travail of
a Daughter of Zion

Rev. Melva Carty

Christian Living Books, Inc.
Largo, MD

Copyright © 2023 Melva Carty

All rights reserved under the international copyright law. No part of this book may be reproduced or transmitted in any form or by any means, electronic or mechanical, including photocopying, recording, or by any information storage and retrieval system, without the express, written permission of the publisher or the author. The exception is reviewers, who may quote brief passages in a review.

Christian Living Books, Inc.
christianlivingbooks.com
We bring your dreams to fruition.

ISBN 9781562295899

Scripture quotations marked (ESV) are taken from The Holy Bible, English Standard Version®, Copyright © 2001 by Crossway, a publishing ministry of Good News Publishers. Scripture quotations marked (KJV) are taken from the from the King James Version of The Holy Bible in the public domain. Scripture quotations marked (MSG) are taken from THE MESSAGE, Copyright © by Eugene H. Peterson 1993, 1994, 1995, 1996, 2000, 2001, 2002. Used by permission of NavPress Publishing Group. Scripture quotations marked (NASB) are taken from the New American Standard Bible®, Copyright © 1960, 1962, 1963, 1968, 1971, 1972, 1973, 1975, 1977, 1995 by The Lockman Foundation. Scripture quotations marked (NKJV) are taken from the New King James Version, Copyright © 1982 by Thomas Nelson, Inc. All rights reserved.

DEDICATION

This book is dedicated to my loving grandmother Edna Carty (May her soul rest in peace), my mother Rosetta Carty, my two children, Niacka Tom-Sahr and Al-Malik Forrest, and my loving grandson Gabriel Joel Tom-Sahr—who are my rocks.

A rock is someone who is consistently there for me. They are the people who pick me up and put a smile on my face. They also give me a reason to continue and forge ahead (my definition).

ACKNOWLEDGMENTS

First and foremost, I thank and acknowledge my heavenly Father, my precious Saviour Jesus Christ, and my darling Holy Spirit for inspiring me to write this book.

Many thanks to all who assisted me in the development of "She has risen from the ashes." A special thanks to my dear aunts, Carlene Carty-Gillion and Nola Carty (may her soul rest in peace) for pouring into me since my childhood. Their constant love, support, humility, and obedience have been a blessing and have allowed me to help people globally. I also thank my cousin, Paulette Liburd, who continually poured into me and ensured I had clothing. Thanks also to my cousin, Andrea Williams, who made sure I had my hair done well and beautifully.

FOREWORD

Firstly, Rev. Carty is a woman of integrity who commands great respect and honour. I have seen her take time out to speak to people from different walks of life in church, on social media, on her radio show, or by writing cards. This has served her in the manner that she is accorded the same respect she gives to others, whether in the church or the community.

Church hurt is something the church does not really speak about. A lot of people suffer from it, but they do not know it's a real thing. I believe it is something that the church should take time to address and teach people the ramifications of. There must be a consciousness that church hurt does not just affect the congregation but the clergy too. The clergy/ministers suffer from it mainly in silence because of pride. They do not want their congregation to see how this brings them to a vulnerable place.

This book is a project that I welcome wholeheartedly. I know it will shed more light on the cross the church is carrying. The topic of church hurt is basically taboo in the Black church. Some clergy struggle to admit they are suffering from this hurt. The young people who want to earnestly serve God are suffering through it too. I have also seen elders in the church go through this and are unable to identify that they are experiencing church hurt.

The release of this book, at this time, will not only open the eyes of the church about church hurt but it will serve to bring the church together. I also see this book as a catalyst that will enable those hurt to acknowledge, admit, and heal. With this as a start, it will also work at a higher level to unify the body of Christ.

People can expect to find lessons and testimonials in this book that give them an opportunity for reconciliation with themselves, their neighbors, communities, and the rest of the world.

As a bishop in the church, I look forward to the launch of this book, and say thank you to Rev. Melva Carty for looking out for the church and the community. These writings will bring healing to people and the nation, especially our young people in the church.

> The Lord is near to the brokenhearted and saves those who are crushed in spirit. (Psalm 34:18 NASB)

Thank you, Rev. Carty!

–Bishop Dr. Wayne Graham

I have the privilege of calling Rev. Melva Carty my little sister from another mother. What I love about my sister is that she is a kingdom woman and all that she does is to focus on the kingdom and working the kingdom way. She is…
- a woman of faith
- a woman of the Word, and
- a woman of integrity and virtue.

My sister is very loyal, supportive, encouraging, and loving. I love the sense of family values that she possesses. I am a family-oriented person, and I really appreciate this virtue in her. I love her plain-speaking, no-nonsense demeanor and straight-to-the-point persona. Whenever an issue arises, my sister says to me, "TJ, if I am wrong, tell me I am wrong." This is so that she can apologize in the event of her actually being wrong. She operates from a place of total transparency and there is comfort in that.

I also respect the fact that if I tell her something, she keeps my confidence. As ministers, we always have people confiding in us, but we never really have that person to confide in. This is usually because our fellow ministers will use what we have confided about as sermon fodder.

Church hurt is something I have faced on so many different levels. This happened to the point that whenever the minister went to the pulpit to preach, I would walk out of the church and sit by the wall until the service was over. In hindsight, I realize that I was standing in judgement because of how they were making me feel: unappreciated, rejected, and never good enough. Because of this, I can truly relate to the topic of church hurts.

I thank God that my sister had the courage to tell this story. I believe it is a timely ministry tool, and I know there are many Christians who have been crippled by the actions of the many "hirelings." I also believe we are the only army that shoots our wounded people.

I believe this book permits people to express the hidden pain and hurts the church has caused them. It is also a license that allows people to be open about areas of their lives that have been buried and hidden. One of the things hurt has caused people to do is have shame. People are hiding behind shame that does not belong to them. Out of loyalty and respect, people have walked and hidden in this shame. But today, after reading this book, they will be loosed from the shame.

> But those who wait on the Lord shall renew their strength; They shall mount up with wings like eagles, they shall run and not be weary, they shall walk and not faint. (Isaiah 40:31 NKJV)
>
> –Rev. Thomas Joseph

I would describe Melva as a go-getter. This is because whatever she sets her mind to do, she will not stop until she achieves her goal. She is tenacious, aggressive, and has a "take a no-prisoner" approach to life. I have been privileged to be a part of her life, and I have seen her refuse to take no for an answer. It was quite evident from the onset that Melva was destined to be a trailblazer and an integral part of the movement of those that champion God's cause. Part of my reason for this assessment of Melva is because, in my youth, I witnessed her interest in the things of God. I would always play the preacher, but she would always volunteer to be a testifier or play the tambourine and pray. This entire activity was a mock-up we genuinely thought was playtime and that we were copying what we saw the adults do. But no, God had us in His school of service.

Church hurt, wow, there are so many things I could say, but I have noticed that every Christian has either faced it or they are well on their way to facing it. Church hurt is painful, shameful, disgraceful, and at its worst sinful. In my opinion, this is the main tool Satan uses to destroy the body of Christ because more often than not, he uses the same people in the church to hurt their brethren as was the case with Melva. Amidst all the hurt Melva endured and encountered and even though she was knocked down, she refused to stay down in the situational ashes. Rather, she bounced back with renewed hope and vigor.

With the writing of this book, Melva is breaking the vow of silence on this topic of church hurt. She has allowed the Lord to use her as a voice for voiceless people who are locked in the prison of church hurt. People are scared to open up because they fear the repercussions. Therefore, this book allows them to gain the confidence to expose this evil.

This book is a book of deliverance, delivering the saints of God from the clutches of this evil monster. With deliverance will come forgiveness, healing, and then restoration will take place, and lastly, reciprocity because they will reciprocate what they have received.

The readers of this book can expect a life-changing message with guidance and direction to get out of the situations that plague them. You will be able to see Melva's victory and be encouraged that if the Lord could make a way of escape for her, He will do it for you also.

With this book, you will come to a realization that God has supplied the strength for us to strive and rise again.

This book is not just to be read as an academic exercise. It will be a conduit and catalyst to spark a change in how church is done. I believe this book is a game changer and life changer that has come at the right time through the inspiration of the Holy Spirit for the saints. Melva was knocked down but not knocked out.

In conclusion, your beginning does not determine your ending and this piece is the game-changer.

> Though your beginning was insignificant, yet your end will increase greatly. (Job 8:7 NASB)
> –HE The Hon. Rev. Ranford J. Queeley DKE, MTh

CONTENTS

Introduction. xv

Chapter 1 – Come on the Journey. 17

Chapter 2 – The Power of Persistence 25

Chapter 3 – She Walks in Victory 41

Chapter 4 – Faithful in Prayer 45

Chapter 5 – The Power of Perseverance 49

About the Author. 53

INTRODUCTION

I wrote this book because for a long time, I went to church and met every expectation I was meant to, but spiritually, I felt dead. A lot of stuff was happening that needed to be addressed, but the leadership felt I was not in good standing to do so. I knew this was in error, but on the other hand, I respected the man (pastor) I believed Jesus had put as the shepherd over the congregation at the time. But I questioned whether he truly was the shepherd or a hireling.

All the activities I participated in and the roles I had to play in the church became chores. Every time I partook in them, I felt like I had a festering wound in me that was oozing sorrow and making me unhappy and uncomfortable.

I decided to go to the Bible institute. For the first time, I confidently and comfortably allowed my eyes to open and see what was. I realised the ministers were talking the talk, but they were not walking the walk. Yet again, when I attempted to raise my observation, I was told it was not my place, and I was not in good standing to give my observation. This made me question:

- What does "in good standing" mean?
- What does being in good standing have to do with my observations?
- Why wasn't I in good standing?

The entire situation got to a point where mud was slung. As much as it did not stick, the impact was felt. And for the first time, I understood I was right in the middle of experiencing church hurt.

CHAPTER 1

COME ON THE JOURNEY

Train up a child in the way he should go, and when he is old he will not depart from it. (Proverbs 22:6 NKJV)

I was born on an island shaped like a guitar called St. Kitts in the West Indies. I was raised in the parish of Trinity in a village called Palmetto Point. Our parish consisted of four villages namely Challengers, Boyds, West Farm, and Palmetto Point.

As small as my Parish is, it is blessed with an immense and beautiful history and culture. In Challengers, we have a place called Bloody River, which is also called Bloody Point. This was the place the Caribs and Arawaks fought and the bloodshed there made it seem as if the river just flowed blood. The river flowed down to a point where the bloody river, fresh water, and the sea met. This point was called Bloody Point.

Right in this area, we have what is called the Challengers Recreation ground with a track and cricket and football fields. It was a place where people from the surrounding villages came to play sports. We would take time out of our days to be there enjoying a fun time with friends and engaging in friendly competitions.

Boyds is home to the Fairview Inn Great House and Botanical Garden Hotel. The hotel is based at the summit of Ottley's Mountain (Ottley's Level). Some people call it Level. Built in the 18th Century, the great house has stood the test of time. We would take school trips there to see what it was and its history. This was also used as a landmark in our geography lessons. What really amazed me, at the time, was having to pass across the train tracks to get to the other side. These tracks were used by the locomotives to transport sugarcane for sugar production.

West Farm is where the French River is and the place that the French occupied. They tilled the land and engaged in other activities. In the West Farm Mountains, we have the Hazel Mountain and the Hole Forest where the movie *Missing in Action* starring Chuck Norris was filmed in 1984. West Farm also had a place called Duporte. This place was also famous for being a loading area for all the sugar cane that came from the plantation and had to be transported for sugar production. We would visit this place often to have our fill of sugarcane and found the entire operation fascinating.

A VICTORIOUS COMMUNITY

Palmetto Point or Point Town was my village. I learned in school it was the first town to be established in St. Kitts. My alma mater was first named Trinity Parish Anglican School.

Chapter 1 ■ Come on the Journey

The name was later changed to Trinity All-Age School and then Trinity Government School. It is now named Bronte Welsh Primary School and is an integral feature of my village.

The Ottley's Mountain (Ottley's Level), which I mentioned earlier, was also shared by my village. The fishermen applied their trade in this area and agricultural endeavours were also done on quite a commercial scale. The Point is home to the first church in the parish which was the Methodist Church. My village is also home to the Jewish cemetery, and it still has the tombstones to date. The first local Governor Sir Beech Allen was a product of my village too and boy, did that make us preen with pride.

Growing up in this parish, there was nothing but love, joy, and the unspeakable fullness of glory. I just loved and looked forward to the morning. The breeze, essence, and ambience woke me up and welcomed me to every new day. Near where I lived was a bakery. I would smell the freshly baked goods every morning and that brought such a comfort to my soul.

I was the only girl in my household and most of my cousins were males. These men were very protective of me and even when I did wrong, they stood to my defence. I also remember them protecting me from the boys in other communities. They would defend me in public but chasten me in private when we got home.

I had to wake up early each morning to take the goats out to pasture, feed my chickens, and sweep the yard with a coconut branch cut out to do the work of a broom. I did all this work before I headed to the Trinity School that was up the hill from my home. Even with all this, it was imperative that I got to school before the school bell rung.

If I was ever late for school, I had to open the palm of my hands to get a few lashes for tardiness. What was ironic and funny is that the headmistress who meted out this harsh punishment (in my adolescent mind) was my cousin. People's eyes were always on me at school because I loved to advocate for others and myself.

At the weekend, I was to avail myself of cooking lessons. I had to wash all my laundry by hand and iron it. It was a wholistic sort of education. I learnt how to starch, darn and sew. I was also taught how to clean, cook on coal, the stove, and firewood but because a lot of respect and honour was put on doing things the traditional way, the preferred form of teaching was the firewood. Having learnt all this, I used the coal method most. I had to go to the community pipe to fetch water, which I then carried on the top of my head. I was also taught to respect and honour everyone I met, and I gave my greeting in every situation I found myself.

> *I loved to advocate for others and myself.*

When it came to academics and extra-curricular activities such as spelling bees and Mathletics (math competitions), folk dances (My cousins say I was great at as we reminisce on those wonderful moments.), talent shows, I was always selected as a group leader for my group. We would have Walk-a-thon competitions where we had to walk around the whole island and the winner would get a trophy.

To this day, I still have all the great memories I had from being awarded for winning. My community was always victorious, and we even entered a carnival troupe competition that we won too. This particular victory put us on the map and even though my village was small, it was *tallowah* (meaning, even though you are small you have a champion's heart).

FRONT AND FORWARD

On Sunday mornings I had to go to the Methodist church in Challengers and, in the evenings, we went to the Good Tidings Gospel Hall known throughout St. Kitts and Nevis as the Boyds Gospel Hall. This Gospel Hall was in the village called Boyd's and the lead Pastor was Mr. Morrell, an Englishman who journeyed as a missionary to St. Kitts. His associate pastor was Hugh Vaughn also known as Pollie.

Even at the church, I was chosen to lead in many social activities: Bible reading, Christmas and Easter skits, church poetry, and the memorization of Bible verses. My Sunday school teacher always put me front and forward in these activities. And I often wondered why. Why me? One day, I took the initiative and went to her home after getting my Christmas assignment to ask her why I got the honour of leading every activity. She simply smiled and looked at me with eyes of wisdom. But now, as I have grown older and kept in contact with her, she has begun to unpack that smile of wisdom. She told me she saw my potential and there was something special in me. What I didn't realise at the time was that God was preparing me to be a trailblazer.

> *God was preparing me to be a trailblazer.*

I left St. Kitts when I was in 6th grade because my family had to relocate to St. Thomas, U.S. Virgin Islands. It was one of the saddest moments of my life. I would frequently visit St. Thomas with my grandmother, but this time, I was going there permanently.

As sad as this move was for me, I found it very beneficial. It piqued my interest because I learnt several new things and the teaching method was different. In St. Kitts, I was taught the British way of writing and in St. Thomas, I was taught the American way. Even mathematics was taught differently. I found all these glaring differences exciting and wonderful. To this day, this experience puts a smile on my heart and face.

RAISING THE FLAG HIGH

When I attended school in St. Thomas, I found it humorous and comforting because the majority of my teachers were from my home country St. Kitts. This allowed me to settle and acclimatise better and in a comfortable manner. I knew they understood me and the culture of my country. I had to continue shining and raising the flag of my country high in this new environment.

It also helped that these teachers knew my mother and family, so I couldn't play fast and loose in any situation. That security blanket was a comfort to me because it kept me on the straight and narrow and from engaging in negative activities.

My grandmother always told me, "Glamma, the sky is not the limit. Continue to shine." She always encouraged and motivated me to do well in all spheres of my life, especially education. She made sure all my school implements were provided. Grandma was my rock. She also took it upon herself to ensure while I was getting fed educationally, I had the spiritual education of the church feeding me too.

God has graced me academically with all these experiences in St. Kitts, St. Thomas, and even in college in the United States. This deeply ingrained discipline allowed me to ambitiously get an associate degree, two bachelor's degrees, and a master's degree, and I am currently doing my PhD in Theology.

> *The sky is not the limit. Continue to shine.*

I am deeply committed and have a servant's heart for Jesus Christ. I have a passion to see God's people live, achieve and be what God says He wants them to be. I believe in my service, I exemplify the mandate given by Jesus Christ, which is found in the Gospel of Matthew:

> And Jesus came and spoke to them, saying, "All authority has been given to Me in heaven and on earth. Go therefore and make disciples of all the nations, baptizing them in the name of the Father and of the Son and of the Holy Spirit, teaching them to observe all things that I have commanded you; and lo, I am with you always, even to the end of the age." Amen.
> (Matthew 28:18-20 NKJV)

CHAPTER 2

THE POWER OF PERSISTENCE

For I know the thoughts that I think toward you, says the Lord, thoughts of peace and not of evil, to give you a future and a hope. (Jeremiah 29:11 NKJV)

In 2013, I believed my life was over. I thought death had come because of an accusation and a slandering of my character. Because of the character assignation against me she had people believing her. That was very painful for me because I had high regards for those people she spoke to. I could not believe that their will fall for that deception but they did.

During my son's graduation from high school in 2017, I heard the Lord tell me to write the book.

> He also spoke this parable: "A certain man had a fig tree planted in his vineyard, and he came seeking fruit on it and found none. Then he said to the keeper of his vineyard, 'Look, for three years I have come seeking

fruit on this fig tree and find none. Cut it down; why does it use up the ground?' But he answered and said to him, 'Sir, let it alone this year also, until I dig around it and fertilize it. And if it bears fruit, well. But if not, after that you can cut it down.'" (Luke 13:6-9 KJV)

I heard a still voice saying to me, "I will raise you up from the ashes." During this time, I was going through a situation in the church. I had this misguided notion that because members had been in church for many years they were living godly lives. I went through this period of my life with my head held high because I knew the sun was going to shine on me again; I was confident God was with me. The Lord told me not to worry. He said, "You are My child; hold your head up high and smile."

During those six months, it was not easy, but I knew the sun was shining. The Lord told me weeping may endure for a night but joy cometh in the morning (Psalm 30:5).

When there is a conversation about church hurt, I can tell you. The hurt started from the head, filtered down to the congregation, and finally, to the last rung in the church.

As a woman of God in the church, when you stand up for righteousness and holiness, people will not like you. They will always fight against you. If I had not been humble and obedient in my walk with God, I would have backslidden. As a woman of God, you must stand on the word of God regardless of what you are going through keep standing. Because of my relationship with God,

> *Regardless of what you are going through keep standing.*

I was able to overcome all obstacle and dig my anchor deeper and stand my ground. I was hearing the voice of God clearly, so I had the confidence to stand. Jesus said in (John 10:27-28 NKJV) "My sheep listen to my voice; I know them, and they follow me. I give them eternal life, and they shall never perish; no one will snatch them out of my hand."

IN GOOD STANDING

I was told I was not in good standing with the church because I stood up for righteousness. When I asked why I was not in good standing, those in charge could not answer the question. For six months they never spoke to me. I was stripped of every position in the church but that did not stop me from serving my God. As a matter of fact, in the church setting, the language is called back benching.

I was called all kinds of unfathomable words, and some of the leaders who I respected in the church disappointed me terribly. God showed me that even though it was a personal attack this is about people jockeying for position in church. The people were not focusing on doing the will of God, there was only focusing on where they wanted to be.

I could not believe they were the ones who spoke badly about me. However, the following two scriptures reminded me that the people in times past spoke ill of Jesus. Why would people not speak ill of me? I was just a woman of God.

> You do the deeds of your father." Then they said to Him, "We were not born of fornication; we have one Father—God." (John 8:41 NKJV)

> And when the Sabbath had come, He began to teach in the synagogue. And many hearing Him were astonished, saying, "Where did this Man get these things? And what wisdom is this which is given to Him, that such mighty works are performed by His hands! Is this not the carpenter, the Son of Mary, and brother of James, Joses, Judas, and Simon? And are not His sisters here with us?" So they were offended at Him. But Jesus said to them, "A prophet is not without honor except in his own country, among his own relatives, and in his own house." Now He could do no mighty work there, except that He laid His hands on a few sick people and healed them. And He marveled because of their unbelief. Then He went about the villages in a circuit, teaching. (Mark 6:2-6 NKJV)

These are the members I sat in the congregation with Sunday after Sunday, and we lifted holy hands together; I heard them give their testimonies of the many years they had been in the church, but when it came to righteousness, they could not stand. They would overlook the abuse of a church member by others, including church members, instead of addressing it.

NATHANIEL'S QUESTION

One time, I overheard a sister say about me, "She will never come to nothing." That broke my heart, but I girded up my loins, and I called my cousin and told him everything that had been said. I reminded him of John 1:46 when Nathaniel said, "Can anything good come out of Nazareth?" Lo and behold, here I am achieving and being who God wants me to be.

This question Nathaniel asked is a confirmation Jesus Christ truly was the fulfilment of all the Scriptures. When Samuel went to anoint David, he had an image in his mind of who was deserving of the appointment but alas, that was not so with God. Until David was presented, the Lord said no to everybody else. He said yes to David, and the next time God says yes is with the Son of David, Jesus Christ. When man rejects you, God projects you, and He prepares a table for you before your enemies.

> *When man rejects you, God projects you.*

They were led astray and became weak for they had not known the Word of God.

> But you, O man of God, flee these things and pursue righteousness, godliness, faith, love, patience, gentleness. (1 Timothy 6:11 NKJV)

One Sunday while in church, the Holy Spirit spoke to me and said, "Woman of God, keep focused, for I am with you. I will uphold your right hand. Your help does not come from men and women; it comes from Me your heavenly Father." Tears ran down my face, and I just began to worship God.

It was not easy going to church every Sunday. When I walked in, every eye was on me from the pulpit to the pew.

ENCOURAGE YOURSELF IN THE LORD

The psalmist (David) in Psalm 130 said we must encourage ourselves in the Lord. When I rose in the morning, I would praise God. I prayed myself up and walked boldly into the church, down the centre isles every Sunday and took my seat in row number seven, seat four or five.

I asked the Lord to keep me during these services. I said, "Daddy Jesus, You know my heart, but why do You have me worshipping You in this place?" Immediately, I heard a voice tell me to look at John 4:24, "God is Spirit: and they that worship him must worship him in spirit and truth."

I love the Lord and truly looked forward to church every Sunday. This Zion daughter would dress up to please Jehovah, who is my provider and comforter. So, when it came to giving, I took joy in bringing my tithes and offerings to the Lord. I would walk with grace and keep my head up high.

Church hurt is not easy, but if God is for you, who can be against you? When God has selected you, it does not matter who else has rejected or neglected you. God's favour overrides all opposition, and you are the winner.

God's favour overrides all opposition.

Things were happening in the church that needed to be addressed. Jesus said, "Do not quit; it is too soon to quit." God said, "I put you, woman of God, in this church for a season and a purpose."

As children of God, we must realize that God will give us a second chance when we make covenants with Him, promise to be faithful, and walk in obedience to the Word, especially when we are living Christ-centered lives.

We must not be quick to tear down each other without knowing the facts. Proverbs 6:16-19 admonishes us not to give up on each other too quickly. Sad to say, it was much easier to communicate with unsaved folks than saints in the church. But my Daddy Jesus was pulling me up from the ashes. He said, "Woman of God, you will rise again." I heard the small, still voice telling me, "I am going to take you places you have never been before, for you will spread the gospel." The best teaching comes from the Holy Spirit. We must see the truth of God in His Word.

We must get to that place where the truth is as stated in the following verse:

> Be diligent to present yourself approved to God as a worker who does not need to be ashamed, accurately handling the word of truth. (2 Timothy 2:15 NASB)

It is not about us; it is about the Word of God.

Jesus said, "Melva, my daughter, rise up from the ashes go out and spread the good news of Me (Jesus) as it's written:

> Go ye therefore, and teach all nations, baptizing them in the name of the Father, and of the Son, and of the Holy Ghost: Teaching them to observe all things whatsoever I have commanded you: and, lo, I am with you always, even unto the end of the world. Amen.
> (Matthew 28:19-20 KJV)

Take the restrictions off yourself for I do not have any restrictions on you. Do not let the naysayers or frenemies place any restrictions on you." I said, "Lord, thank You for loving me first. Thank You for saving a wretch like me."

I was once told that I am not like others in the church because I stand up for what I believe in: living right. I was also told I am a strong-willed person. I replied, "If God is for me, who can be against me? I am not angry with you because I know Abba is not angry with me for standing firm. All glory and honour belong to Him."

CUT AND PRUNED

I was told boldly in the church that I would no longer read the Scriptures, pray, or perform in any capacity as I used to. "This is a season of repentance." This made me go home to search myself and my heart to see where I went wrong because I believed that if this was my punishment, I had to figure out my crime. I knew there and then that I had to come to a place of repentance in Christ Jesus. I also did not want to throw people under the bus or look as if I was bitter because it really was not about that.

On that Sunday, driving home from church, I heard that still small voice say, "My Zion daughter, please read Jeremiah 29:11."

> For I know the thoughts that I think toward you, saith the Lord, thoughts of peace, and not of evil, to give you an expected end.

God said, "I am molding you for My will and purpose. Not your will but My will."

Not your will but My will.

I read that scripture every day, and as soon as I rose, I gave God thanks for a second chance. I almost died spiritually. I thanked Him for a second chance of mercy, and as my keeper, He had every right to cut and prune me for this journey.

Prayer warrior, God shows us mercy every day. He has the right to cut us down and pull us up. It is a two-edged sword:

> The Lord knoweth how to deliver the godly out of temptations, and to reserve the unjust unto the day of judgement to be punished. (2 Peter 2:9 KJV)

My impetus for this book is to tell someone who is reading it if you see your brother or sister going the wrong way show kindness:

> So when they continued asking Him, He lifted up Himself, and said unto them, he that is without sin among you, let him first cast a stone at her. (John 8:7 KJV)

Be yourself and stay strong in God's Word. Stand for what you believe in.

PRAYER

Lord, I thank You for ordering my steps on holy ground. Thank You for the second chance. Please forgive me for not seeking You more. Lord, when the churches repent as You said in Leviticus Chapter 19, "deliverance will come."

Jesus is the dresser in the vineyard, not your pastor or leader in the church who is playing church and not hearing from God.

> **PRAYER**
>
> Lord, I declare changes in the churches. You know the churches by name. It is time for the church to be the church and not be like the seven churches in Revelation 1:11: "Saying, I am Alpha and Omega, the first and the last: and, What thou seest, write in a book, and send it unto the seven churches which are in Asia; unto Ephesus, and unto Smyrna, and unto Pergamos, and unto Thyatira, and unto Sardis, and unto Philadelphia, and unto Laodicea."

God doesn't care how many tithes or offerings you bring to the church, how long you have been a member of a church, or whether you are the builder or founder of the church. The question is are you living a Christ-centred life that is pleasing to God?

> **PRAYER**
>
> Lord, I declare changes in the church, may we truly come into repentance and ask for Your mercy as it is written:
>
> > He that dwelleth in the secret place of the most High shall abide under the shadow of the Almighty.
> > (Psalm 91:1 KJV)
>
> > And I say also unto thee, That thou art Peter, and upon this rock I will build my church; and the gates of hell shall not prevail against it.
> > (Matthew 16:18 KJV)

Secondly, I was told that I was not fit to be a leader because I was not from the "island of Jamaica." As I continued my journey with God, He told me, "My Zion daughter, I want you to keep yourself focused, for a position in the church doesn't make you. I am going to make you a servant leader, for you have the heart of a servant leader."

KINGDOM LOVE

You are going to do things the King's way with kingdom principles and pure kingdom love.

> Now before the Feast of the Passover, when Jesus knew that His hour had come that He should depart from this world to the Father, having loved His own who were in the world, He loved them to the end. And supper being ended, the devil having already put it into the heart of Judas Iscariot, Simon's son, to betray Him, Jesus, knowing that the Father had given all things into His hands, and that He had come from God and was going to God, rose from supper and laid aside His garments, took a towel and girded Himself. After that, He poured water into a basin and began to wash the disciples' feet, and to wipe them with the towel with which He was girded. (John 13:1-5 NKJV)

Jesus told me that He came to Earth and took on the form of humanity in order to experience what it means to be human. That is what incarnation means. It ultimately means the oneness of God and humanity. God came down and became one of us, 100 percent God yet 100 percent man. Man, who had to be born, who had to live off the land, who had to work by the sweat of His brow so that He could have food, shelter, and clothing. Man who had to suffer temptations, trials, and suffering.

Jesus did not come to have others serve Him but instead, as John Chapter 13 spells out so vividly, Jesus came to pick up a towel and serve others. He said, "Even so, do, My Zion daughter." Even though it is hurting, you must continuously show love.

Without love for others, everything is meaningless. Most people have the misconception that serving God is about popularity, being in the spotlight, being recognized, or getting a pat on the back. Serving God is not about self-promotion, it is about lifting up the name of Jesus. As John the Baptist said, "I must decrease while Christ increases in me."

> *Without love for others, everything is meaningless.*

Yes, you must serve God with a clean heart and a heart of gratitude. Serve Him with love and compassion. Serve as royalty with loyalty. Serve with faithfulness, and remember when you are serving, you are serving unto God, so your reward is not coming from man, but it is coming from God.

KINGDOM PRINCIPLES

I have noticed that many Christians do not know the kingdom principles because many churches are not teaching them anymore. If you want to be happy, to live an abundant life, to live rather than exist, if you want to be remembered after you are gone from this world, then pour out your life into others.

Too many leaders in today's church are more concerned about what everybody else is doing or not doing. They make excuses why it's somebody else's job to do the work, and wait for others to get the job done. It should be our desire to serve who we can when we can. But many Christians do not want to serve from the bottom; they want to serve from the top.

Jesus served from the bottom. He washed the disciple's feet. You can be a pastor, and not be a servant. You can be a song leader and not be a servant. You can be a pianist and not be a servant. You can be a deacon, and not be a servant. You can be a Sunday school teacher and servanthood is far from you. You can hold any office, any title within the church and still not be a servant. However, if you want to be better than having a job title, if you want to do more than just occupy an office within the church, you must humble yourself and become a servant.

> *Jesus served from the bottom.*

We need an attitude of servanthood. Jesus gives us an example of a good shepherd and a servant. The good shepherd will leave the ninety-and-nine and look for one. That is what a good shepherd and a good servant will do. Servanthood is an action, not just a word. If you are a servant, you will demonstrate your actions and see the fruits of those actions. To be a servant you must love. The Godhead itself, the Trinity, exhibits a servant relationship. Jesus serves the Father. Jesus quotes from the prophet Isaiah in Mathew 12:18. In that passage, Jesus says that He fulfils the role of a servant: "Behold my servant that I have chosen."

A STRONG ANCHOR

If I did not have a strong anchor during this storm, my ship would have lost anchor. As it states in Hebrews 6:19, in times like these, I truly needed an anchor. My trust was and is in God's Word. I took the Bible as my sword, and I was truly anchored in my Saviour.

I faced a lot of jealousy in the church and due to my training as a child, I could not help but do things excellently. I did not expect serving in that manner would give rise to all these ill effects. Brethren, I was never jealous nor was I exposed to it. So, I struggled to maneuver through it. But God was the strength of my heart and my portion forever.

Be encouraged knowing that the same Holy Spirit who worked through Moses, Joshua, Gideon, Daniel, Peter, and so many other great men and women of the Bible is the same Holy Spirit who is working through you. God does not change!

> Jesus Christ is the same yesterday, today, and forever.
> (Hebrews 13:8 NKJV)

The same power that split the Red Sea, dried the river Jordan, and shut the lion's mouth, is living inside you. When you grasp this, you'll realise that the way God uses you to demonstrate His glory is limitless. He will do the impossible in your life as you, too, like me, rise from the ashes.

During my journey, I counted my blessings and named them one by one. God reminded me that my hope was built on nothing less than Jesus' blood and His righteousness. It is not what happens to us on the outside. It is what is inside of us.

We should always honour the great God for what He is doing for us. Hebrews Chapter 6 is one of my favourite scriptures because it begins with a warning of life and ends with blessed assurance that I am faithful, and I trust in God.

As children of God, we must know what a true Christian relationship with Him is. It is the Lord who gives and the Lord who takes away. My identity is in Christ, not in man or woman. I have a hope that is built on nothing else but Jesus Christ and His righteousness. On Christ the solid rock I stand, all other ground is sinking sand. I had to study the Word to learn it for myself.

I have overcome and risen from the ashes. Your leaders cannot ride out your storm or usher you into heaven. Our heavenly Father has given us a weapon on how to reach heaven: the ministry of prayer.

> *No man is greater than his prayer life.*

Thank You, Lord, for International Bread of Life Ministry Global and Church Without Walls Global.

I have learnt that no man is greater than his prayer life. Any leader in the ministry who is not praying is playing the people, and the members who are not praying are straying away from God.

God answers prayer. Therefore, there is no door He cannot open. He opened Bartimaeus' blind eyes. He opened Elizabeth's barren womb. He opened the Red Sea for the children of Israel and terminated 430 years of slavery.

PRAYER

Lord Jesus, as I rise this day, let all angels of help and mercy shall rise and work for me. Let every door of blessings, joy, happiness, prosperity, salvation, and every good thing shut against me be opened for me.

Tell yourself God raised Melva Carty from the ashes, and He can do it for me.

CHAPTER 3

SHE WALKS IN VICTORY

> For the Lord your God is he who goes with you to fight for you against your enemies, to give you the victory.
> (Deuteronomy 20:4 ESV)

I was at a place where I had to know who Melva Carty was in Christ, and what I have received from Him. The Spirit resides in our spirits from the day we are born again (Galatians 5:22).

God wanted me to live a life of faith and victory. He told me I will face tribulations, trials, and temptations of many kinds.

On September 27, 2017, I was accepted to First Baptist of Glenarden's Divine Discipleship for Sisters. God spoke to me that evening while sitting in my car. He told me this is where you are going to walk in your victory. While attending this seminary class for thirteen months, I grew in God. I spent more time in the Bible and discovered that King David's words were true:

> Your word is a lamp to my feet and a light to my path.
> (Psalm 119:105 NKJV)

Apostle Paul's words were also true when he said:

> For the word of God is living and powerful, and sharper than any two-edged sword, piercing even to the division of soul and spirit, and of joints and marrow, and is a discerner of the thoughts and intents of the heart.
> (Hebrew 4:12 NKJV)

A REASON AND A PURPOSE

It was not an easy word that Jesus spoke to me during orientation. He said, "My Zion daughter, I brought you here for a reason and a purpose." But I did not understand what He meant. I had to go through assessments to pass the class: The Disciple's Cross, The Disciple's Personality, The Disciple's Victory, and The Disciple's Mission.

I had to know my foundation scripture:

> Then He said to them all, "If anyone desires to come after Me, let him deny himself, and take up his cross daily, and follow Me. (Luke 9:23 NKJV)

These assessments equipped me with the authority of God's Word and the ability to walk in victory. I had to live a Christ-centered life through biblical and practical application to embody the heart of Christ.

Jesus Christ was equipping me for the plan He had for my life. I had to spend time with the Master. I had to live in the Word, pray in faith, fellowship with believers, witness to the world, and minister to others. This truly taught me the disciple's cross.

During my first assessment, I was taught how to hear the voice of God and pray to build a strong relationship with Him. During my prayer time, my faith was unlocked, and I began to grow spiritually. Every time I went to class, I kept on hearing the voice of God telling me to keep walking in my victory and speak the truth of God, for He was with me.

> *This truly taught me the disciple's cross.*

On the day of my first assessment, God visited me in the class. One of my covenant sisters who was sitting next to me experienced the encounter of God and shouted out "Glory!" Jesus said to me, "My Zion daughter, this is just the beginning. I brought you here for a reason, to equip you. Looking around, people are here from different denominations. You cannot fight your spiritual enemies on your own strength but by the divine authority of Jesus Christ."

EQUIPPED FOR SERVICE

My Daddy Jesus equipped me by waking me up every morning at 5:00 a.m. to spend time with Him reading the Word and applying it to myself. In my first assessment, I witnessed the power of God's Word and walked in my victory. My heavenly Father truly used me at Divine Discipleship for Sisters for His glory and equipped me during all my sessions. My covenant sisters and facilitators were always excited when it was time for me to make a presentation. They expressed that their hearts were blessed whenever I did.

I heard a small voice speak to me while sitting in class and waiting for my name to be called so that I could present my assignment. It said, "The fresh anointing has fallen on you. I have equipped you to walk in your victory. Hold your head up high and walk in your season with grace." While I was in the anointing, I told the class that I know my Redeemer lives. I used a red lamp to demonstrate how God had used and equipped me to walk in my victory. I gave my testimony and preached the Word of God. The Lord also told me that I was anointed to win.

That day, God commissioned me to go out and spread the good news. One of my facilitators was a pastor. I didn't know what she had told my classmates when she came into the class, but she kept looking at me and saying, "This sister is a pastor; she is here on a journey from God and has a special anointing on her." She stated that when I open my mouth, she felt the power of God light up the room and a different atmosphere. During my last assessment, I truly felt the fire of the Holy Spirit burning inside of my belly and the hotness in my hands.

CHAPTER 4

FAITHFUL IN PRAYER

Rejoicing in hope, persevering in tribulation, devoted to prayer. (Romans 12:12 NASB)

A John Hagee message, entitled "What is Prayer", really ministered to me. He said, "What is prayer? Prayer is not sending God to run your errands."

A Christian can see more on his knees than he can from his feet. Prayer is not getting God to prepare to do your will. Rather, prayer is getting you to prepare to do God's will. Prayer is the only way to release the supernatural power of God in your life. I will show you great and mighty things that you know not, says the Lord.

Prayer is the key that unlocks the gate to heaven and closes the gate to hell. Prayer does not need proof. Prayer needs practice. God answers prayer, we need to pray and seek God's face.

When my life was empty, I prayed, and God answered my prayer. I am here to tell someone that a prayerless Christian is a weak Christian. A prayerless Christian is a miserable Christian. A prayerless Christian is a Christian who always lives in defeat. A prayerless church is a weak church. A prayerless nation is a defeated nation. A prayerless family will be a divided family. It has been said that a family that prays together stays together.

> Ask, and it will be given to you; seek, and you will find; knock, and it will be opened to you. For everyone who asks receives, and the one who seeks finds, and to the one who knocks it will be opened.
> (Matthew 7:7-8 NASB)

God expects us to pray. God answers prayer. Sometimes I say, "Lord, who is praying for me?" Other times I would ask the Lord for things that were impossible for me to accomplish, but I knew with God, all things are possible if I believe. He showed me great and mighty things that astonished me.

One day, I heard the voice of God tell me to ask Him for anything my heart desired. He told me if I desired healing, a mountain moved, or financial blessing, I only had to ask. He will not withhold any good thing from those who walk uprightly (Psalm 84:11).

He is the Creator, owner of the cattle upon a thousand hills (Psalm 50:10). The earth is His and the fullness thereof, the world, and they that dwell therein (Psalm 24:1-2). In Job 38:4, God asked Job where he was when He laid the foundations of the earth. From these verses, we see the magnificence of God and His creative power. Yet, we can talk to Him through prayer. Prayer is a heavenly currency that is submitted by faith. Prayer gives God permission to intercede on our behalf in our day-to-day lives.

A DIVINE INVITATION

Prayer is a divine invitation that summons the host of heaven to step out of eternity into time. Until we truly pray with understanding and knowledge and pray skillfully, we are praying amiss. Prayer authorizes heaven to enter fair and square into the affairs of men and to act on our behalf. John Wesley said, "God can do nothing to and for humanity until we pray."

> *Prayer gives God permission to intercede on our behalf.*

Prayer is the engine oil that causes a man to be in communication and communion with God. Prayer is a daily necessity for our daily survival. Prayerlessness is the reason why wickedness and wizardry are taking over our countries and churches.

Prayer is the breath of the church. If we stop praying, the church will only exist in the past or become a social event where we only meet. Scripture says we must always pray and not faint. We must pray without ceasing. We must pray strategically and know what we will pray about. Let the Holy Ghost, who is your helper, take you into the secret place and let your request be known unto God.

Prayer is a weapon against your enemies. Through prayer, we break through the spirit realm. Keep your eyes on Jesus by faith and heaven will move at your command.

Joshua prayed for the sun to stand still!

> Then Joshua spoke to the Lord in the day when the Lord delivered up the Amorites before the children of Israel, and he said in the sight of Israel: "Sun, stand still over Gibeon; And Moon, in the Valley of Aijalon." So the sun stood still, And the moon stopped, Till the people had revenge Upon their enemies. Is this not written in the Book of Jasher? So the sun stood still in the midst of heaven, and did not hasten to go down for about a whole day. (Joshua 10:12-13 NKJV)

We can connect to the heavenly realm and dismantle Satan's stronghold. Prayer is a force and weapon that only devoted servants can handle. Faith is the engine oil that connects us to prayer.

CHAPTER 5

THE POWER OF PERSEVERANCE

> And not only this, but we also celebrate in our tribulations, knowing that tribulation brings about perseverance; and perseverance, proven character; and proven character, hope; and hope does not disappoint.
> (Romans 5:3-5a NASB)

In reality, when I write about the idea of PUSH [**P**ray **U**ntil **S**omething **H**appens], I have to admit that a time came after all this adversity when I was hungry for God. This hunger was bordering on starvation, and to some people, it seemed like pride and arrogance.

In my quest to understand this hunger, I realised that it wasn't arrogance, but it was an unyielding love and trust I had in God. There was a difference. I wasn't pushing God, but I was clinging unto Him to fill me.

In all this, I came to a point in my prayer life where PUSH became my way of life. I realised I had to keep at it. I set values in my life and prayer life. I did not allow myself to get weary, complacent, or to complain. I stood as a Zion daughter, and I kept pressing on until I got the answers to the questions, requests, and supplications I made to God. Every day, I was gaining and strengthening my spiritual muscles. I would always pray to God to plant my feet on higher ground.

The analogy that comes to mind when I think of this is that of a pregnant woman on the labour bed. The woman does not stop pushing until she births her baby. That was the tenacity with which I decided to approach this new way of life.

> *I kept pressing on until I got the answers.*

I must admit that all this was elusive until I surrendered all to Him, and when I did, He birthed what is now the International Bread of life Ministry and Church Without Walls Global. As a woman of God, I must say praying without ceasing is crucial. Some people think prayer is a one-off endeavour and that you get what you want there and then. However, prayer is not magic or the act of rubbing the genie out of the proverbial bottle.

When we pray, it's important to stop complaining because this gives the Enemy an even stronger foothold. When we strengthen the Enemy's foothold, we leave ourselves vulnerable to his devices. The only remedy to this is to stay on our knees in prayer and supplication with thanksgiving as that is where our victory is hedged.

SIX NUGGETS TO KEEP UP THE FAITH

1. Pray in faith. (Ephesians 3:20; James 1:6)
2. Pray in the Spirit. (Ephesians 6:18)
3. Pray honestly. (Luke 6:12)
4. Pray in the name of Jesus. (John 14:6)
5. Pray according to the will of God. (1 John 5:14)
6. Fasting and prayer help us in battle. (Matthew 17:21)

As vessels of God, our usefulness determines our faithfulness. Broken vessels are conducive to the power of God being manifested on Earth. I encourage you to seek Him wholeheartedly so He can use you for His glory.

> Be cheerful no matter what; pray all the time; thank God no matter what happens. This is the way God wants you who belong to Christ Jesus to live.
> (1 Thessalonians 5:16-18 MSG)

Brethren, irrespective of any hurt, keep PUSHing, serving, and being encouraged. The Lord is on your case. The difference between a winner and a quitter is that a winner gets up one last time. Make sure at the end of the day you are the winner. People are counting on you to make it so they also have an opportunity to win. Your testimony is the lamp to somebody's feet and a light to their path in Christ Jesus.

Keep PUSHing, serving, and being encouraged.

I Am Anointed to Win!

ABOUT THE AUTHOR

Melva Carty is the Founder and President of International Bread of Life Ministry and Servant Leader/Founder of Church Without Walls Global. She was born on one of the beautiful dual-islands located south of the star-studded highways of St. Barbs just west of Saint John on St. Kitts. She is an Investigator for Adult Protective Services in Prince George County. In addition, she has served as Financial Aid Officer for the College of Dentistry and Financial Aid Coordinator for the Scholarship/Special Awards department at Howard University.

Rev. Carty is the recipient of many accolades. In June 2023, she became the first in Prince George's County to become National Adult Protective Service Association (NAPSA) certified. In 2022, she received the Prince George County Customer Services Award 2022, Thurgood Marshall Scholarship Fund, Inc. Leadership Award, Who's Who Among American College Students, Rutgers University Honorable Mention Academic Achievement Award, and Grace Deliverance International Bible College President Award.

Rev. Carty earned a master's in Social Work from Howard University, a bachelor's degree in Criminal Justice, and Psychology from Rutgers University, and an associate degree in Criminal Justice and Social Science from Essex County College.

The proud mother of two children and one grandchild, she resides in Bowie, Maryland.

CONNECT WITH THE AUTHOR

Twitter: @MelvaCarty
Instagram: @risenfromtheashes2023
Website: www.ibolminstry.org

www.ingramcontent.com/pod-product-compliance
Lightning Source LLC
LaVergne TN
LVHW051512070426
835507LV00022B/3077